W9-ATU-131

Learning to Be Kind and Understand Differences

EMPATHY SKILLS FOR KIDS WITH AD/HD

by Judith M. Glasser, PhD, and Jill Menkes Kushner, MA
illustrated by Charles Beyl

MAGINATION PRESS • WASHINGTON, DC
American Psychological Association

Contents

ST. FRANCIS PUBLIC LIBRARY

3 5249 00125 8930

X 618.928589 G549
35249001258930
40cnf
Glasser, Judith
Learning to be kind and understand
differences : empathy skills for kids
with AD/HD

Learning
to Be Kind
and Understand
Differences

DEC 8 2015

WITHDRAWN

ST. FRANCIS PUBLIC LIBRARY
1230 S. NICHOLSON AVE
ST. FRANCIS, WI 53235
(414) 481-READ (40)

FL-28-2

Text copyright © 2016 by Magination Press, an imprint of the American Psychological Association. Illustrations copyright © 2016 by Charles Beyl. All rights reserved. Except as permitted under the United States Copyright Act of 1976, no part of this publication may be reproduced or distributed in any form or by any means, or stored in a database or retrieval system, without the prior written permission of the publisher.

Published by
Magination Press ®
An Educational Publishing Foundation Book
American Psychological Association
750 First Street NE
Washington, DC 20002

Magination Press is a registered trademark of the American Psychological Association.

For more information about our books, including a complete catalog, please write to us, call 1-800-374-2721, or visit our website at www.apa.org/pubs/magination.

Book design by Susan K. White

Printed by Lake Book Manufacturing, Inc., Melrose Park, IL

Library of Congress Cataloging-in-Publication Data

Glasser, Judith M.
Learning to be kind and understand differences : empathy skills for kids with ad/hd / by Judith M. Glasser, Ph.D. and Jill Menkes Kushner, MA.
pages cm
ISBN 978-1-4338-2043-4 (hbk.) — ISBN 1-4338-2043-9 (hbk.)
ISBN 978-1-4338-2044-1 (pbk.) — ISBN 1-4338-2044-7 (pbk.)
1. Empathy—Juvenile literature. 2. Social skills—Juvenile literature.
3. Attention-deficit-disordered children—Juvenile literature. I. Kushner, Jill Menkes. II. Title.
BF575.E55.G53 2016
618.92'8589—dc23   2015010804

Manufactured in the United States of America

First printing August 2015

10 9 8 7 6 5 4 3 2 1

i 2 1 7 9 1 2 0 4 9

To Parents and Other Helpers

EVERY child is an individual. Children are born with different personalities, abilities, and ways of expressing themselves. If you have more than one child, you have probably noticed—even during pregnancy—that one of them was different from the other. One child may have been very active and kicked a lot, while the other was so quiet that you hardly knew she was there.

As your children developed, they probably showed additional differences; one may have slept through the night early, and the other was still waking up for a snack even as a toddler. As your children become older, you may be aware of even more differences. One of your children may be really good at math, music, or art, while the other may struggle in these areas but excel at reading, writing, or science.

Just like the other ways in which children change over time and show their individuality, they may vary in their ability to understand how others think and feel. Some children understand that other people see things differently than they do and have different feelings than they do.

The ability to understand how another person is thinking and feeling without being told is called *empathy*. There are actually different aspects of what we call empathy:

- the ability to see things from another person's point of view
- the ability to feel what another person is feeling
- the ability to imagine what it might be like to be another person and to put yourself in someone else's shoes

Empathy takes time to develop. The beginning of empathy is when babies first understand that they are separate and different from their parents. If you have the chance, watch a baby look in a mirror while being held by his mom or dad. He might show some confusion as he looks back and forth between the mirror and himself or his parent. This is the beginning of learning about the difference between himself and other people.

As a toddler, he will begin to understand that other people have feelings. In preschool, he may try to comfort a friend who is crying. By age 5 or 6, many children have learned to "read" the nonverbal cues of other people to know how they are feeling. However, as with other milestones of development such as learning to walk and talk, the development of empathy varies from child to child and takes time, teaching, and support. For some children, these skills develop easily and naturally. Others need help. It is for these children that we have written this book.

Some children find that empathy skills are very difficult to learn. For example, your daughter may assume that other people think and feel just like she does. She may not understand that people are different. She may never talk about feelings, so you may be unaware of what she doesn't know!

Some children act as though they have no interest—or they may say they don't care what other people think or feel. For children with AD/HD, learning the skills that are necessary to treat others with empathy and kindness requires some of the very skills with which they have the most difficulty. Having empathy and treating people with kindness requires the ability to stop and think and pay attention to how you feel—and then turn your attention to how someone else might see things and feel—and then remember these thoughts and feelings from different perspectives at the same time! After all that, you need to organize your thoughts and plan a response. This is a tall order for kids with AD/HD. Therefore, as adults, it is our responsibility to begin the conversation. We need to model and teach the basics of empathy to our children.

Understanding how others think and feel is a critical skill for all children to learn. It is a skill they will need, and use, throughout their lives. Someone who has the ability to understand how another person is thinking and feeling can have an easier time controlling her own feelings and being kind to others. After all, if your child understands how a friend thinks and feels, she can put herself in his shoes and understand why he behaved the way he did. If he behaved in a hurtful way, her ability to empathize will help her forgive him or feel less hurt.

Our relationship with others is like a circle that involves a continual exchange of thoughts and feelings. How we think about things affects how we feel about them and how we act toward other people. Then, how we act toward others affects how they think and feel about us, how they treat us, and how we in turn feel.

So, understanding differences and treating other people with kindness may help them to treat us with kindness as well!

Empathy is often confused with compassion, but it is actually quite different. Compassion is more about wanting to help other people— but it does not necessarily involve understanding how they think and feel. For example, if you donate food to a food pantry, you understand that people are hungry, and you are showing compassion. However, you don't necessarily have a true understanding of how those hungry people think and feel.

People who have the ability to be empathetic have more success getting along with others. Empathetic people tend to get along well with classmates and teachers. They have fewer problems in school. As adults, they get along well with co-workers and are more successful at work.

Children with AD/HD can be just as empathetic as other children; they can get along well with classmates and others, they can read body language, and they can talk about their feelings. But for those children with AD/HD who do have trouble getting along with others, these interactions can be challenging. One child may not be able to pay attention to what is happening with others because he is so focused on what's going on inside him. Another child may be easily distracted by the sights and sounds that are going on around him, making it difficult for him to concentrate on thoughts and feelings, whether they are his own or anyone else's.

Some children with AD/HD do not have the language to express what they are feeling: they may not be used to using words like "unhappy" or "confused." And some children aren't aware of—or just don't know—what they are feeling, so it can be hard for them to know what another person is feeling.

In addition to all of these challenges, some children with AD/HD have difficulty understanding non-verbal behaviors. Non-verbal behaviors are facial expressions, body positions, gestures, and the tone of voice that people use when they are talking. In other words, non-verbal behaviors include everything that goes along with the words people say aloud. They can be just as important as words in helping a child understand what people really mean.

Finally, kids with AD/HD are often impulsive. They "leap before they look."

In other words, they talk and act before they have had a chance to think about how what they say and do might affect others.

You can imagine that if a child has trouble paying attention to others, is easily distracted, lacks words to express feelings, does not understand how he feels, cannot read non-verbal behaviors, and is impulsive, he is going to have difficulty understanding how another person is feeling and will likely have problems getting along with others.

This book is intended for parents to read along with their child. Counselors or other professionals who work with children can also make use of this book. It's a good idea to read the chapters in order, since they build upon each other. You might want to pause after each chapter to talk about what you and your child have learned and how it might apply to your child's daily life. Also, children with AD/HD sometimes have trouble concentrating for long periods of time and may need "brain breaks."

Please take the time you and your child need to do the chapter exercises carefully and thoughtfully before moving forward. For instance, it might be helpful to read each chapter on a different day and practice in between. Your child may want to draw or write in the book or keep a separate journal, or she may ask you or her counselor to write for her. Whatever works for your child is the best practice.

We will give your child some ideas to help him recognize and talk about his feelings, as well as recognize and talk about the feelings of other people. We will also give you some ideas for techniques to practice the information that you and your child are learning. After some practice, you will probably come up with your own ideas to expand the range of ways to help your child master the building blocks of empathy.

At some point in your life, you have probably heard someone refer to the sentiments of the Golden Rule, often commonly phrased as "Do unto others as you would have them do unto you." The Golden Rule is a universal concept. In fact, all of the world's major ethical approaches have expressed the Golden Rule in one form or another over the centuries. This rule is about putting empathy into action.

You and your child do not have to belong to a particular culture or observe a particular tradition to begin this important journey of discovering and practicing empathy. Empathy is a skill that your child needs now to succeed at school, at play, and in life. And he will need this ability, ultimately, as an adult—to get along well with others, to establish meaningful and long-lasting relationships, and to succeed in the world.

Just for Kids!

THINK of a time when you felt like you were really getting along well with your friends or family. Maybe you were playing a game, or taking a bike ride, or just sharing a meal or a snack. It felt really good, I bet.

Now, think about another time when you weren't getting along so well. A lot of kids have trouble getting along with other people, and that can certainly be true for kids with AD/HD, too. Do you understand why this might happen? Sometimes this problem happens because you say things and do things without thinking. Then you might accidentally say or do something you didn't mean. In this situation, it would be really nice if you could take it back, wouldn't it?

At times, all kids have trouble getting along with others because they don't understand how other people think and feel. Do you think that everyone sees things just like you? Are you surprised to know that other people might see the exact same situation and think differently than you?

Maybe you understand that people sometimes see things differently. But it can still be really hard for you to tell what other people are thinking and feeling. And it can be even harder when the other person isn't talking, and you have to figure out what he's feeling.

THAT HAT MAKES YOU LOOK FUNNY

There are many ways to figure out how people feel. People's faces often show how they feel. And sometimes the way people talk—not just *what they say*—can give you clues about how they feel.

Think about someone you know at school. Can you tell when he looks happy? Can you see when he's sad or angry? Does he sometimes speak more loudly or softly than usual? Does he sound upset sometimes? Clues like these give you helpful information.

You can only understand how other people feel if you understand your own feelings. Do you know how to talk about what you are feeling inside and how to tell someone else? Do you know the words that describe how your body feels when you have a strong feeling—like being angry, or sad, or glad?

We wrote this book because we really want to help you learn some ways to understand what other people feel. This book can help you get along with other people—your family, your friends, your teammates—everyone you know!

First, we are going to share *ideas* about how to understand someone else's "point of view"—in other words, how someone else thinks and feels—and how another person might see things differently from you.

Next, we will give you some *words* to use to talk about some of your feelings. You will be able to use these words to explain what you are thinking and feeling.

We'll also talk about how to understand what a person is feeling by carefully looking at her face or listening to her voice. We'll give you many ways to practice, so you can become really good at knowing what you feel and what other people feel, too. We'll show you how to understand what it means to be in "someone else's shoes," as well as how to understand their point of view and how they might think and feel.

Next, we'll brainstorm about what might have happened that led someone to have certain feelings. To "brainstorm" means to come up with all the ideas you can think of. The point is to just get your thoughts out of your head and written down! You might need a grown-up to help you with this task.

Everyone—even adults—can become better at getting along with others. We know that you will be able to learn these skills. Think of it as one more thing you're learning, like riding a bike or putting a puzzle together. You can learn to understand more about how you think and feel and act toward other people. You can also learn to understand how other people think and feel and why they might act the way they do.

With these new ideas in your head, you will learn how to treat other people with kindness more of the time. They will probably treat you with kindness more of the time, too. That will feel pretty good!

CHAPTER ONE

What Is Empathy?

EMPATHY is the ability to understand how other people think and feel. It's a skill you can learn, and this book will help you. We will help you understand differences between you and other people and how your actions affect how others think and feel.

What Is Empathy All About?

Here's what empathy involves:

E: Everyone sees things differently.

M: My feelings—I can learn to recognize and label them.

P: Point of view—How I see things affects how I feel. How other people see things affects how they feel.

A: Ask yourself—What clues do I see or hear that show me how another person feels?

T: Treat others the way I want to be treated.

H: How I act affects how other people treat me and how I feel.

Y: Yes—I can put myself in someone else's shoes and understand how they think and feel!

THAT IS EMPATHY!

If you think about how other people think and feel, it can change how you act. In turn, how you act affects how others think and feel—and how they treat you. You will get along better with people when you show empathy.

Let's look at the cartoon at the beginning of this chapter. Take a moment to think about what is happening in this cartoon and talk about it with a grown-up. What do you think the big sister is thinking and feeling?

_____

_____

_____

_____

What do you think the little sister is thinking and feeling?

_____

_____

_____

_____

Here are some ideas we thought of: Think about how each girl sees this situation. The big sister might want to protect her space. Maybe the little sister wants to spend some time with her big sister.

How do you think each girl is feeling? From their faces, it seems like the big sister is mad and the little sister is sad. Do you agree?

What do you think would have happened if the cartoon stopped right there? How do you think the girls would have gotten along for the rest of the day? How would the little sister think and feel about her big sister? How would she treat her?

But then, maybe the older sister looks at the little girl's face and sees that she is sad.

It looks like she thinks about things differently. She thinks to herself that maybe instead of trying to get into her room, her sister just wants to play with her. That changes how she feels. It looks like she is not mad anymore. Then she invites her little sister into her room and asks her to play.

Both of them end up smiling! Now, how do you think the girls will get along the rest of the day? How do you think the little sister will think and feel about her big sister? How will she treat her?

Why Is Empathy Important?

Let's think about the cartoon and the word *empathy*. What are the hidden steps that went on in this cartoon?

E: *Everyone sees things differently.*

The big sister had to understand that her little sister might see the situation differently.

M: *My Feelings—I can learn to recognize and label them.*

The big sister had to understand and label how she was feeling.

P: *Point of view—How I see things affects how I feel. How other people see things affects how they feel.*

The big sister had to put herself in her sister's shoes and think about how she might see the situation differently.

A: *Ask yourself—What clues do I see or hear that show me how another person feels?*

The big sister then had to ask herself about what clues she had about how her sister might be feeling. She may have realized from looking at her sister's face that she felt sad.

T: *Treat others the way I want to be treated.*

Maybe the big sister realized she might not like it if someone talked to her the way she had talked to her sister.

H: *How I act affects how other people treat me and how I feel.*

By inviting her sister to play, her sister probably felt good, and they both had fun instead of being upset.

Y: *Yes—I can put myself in someone else's shoes and understand how they think and feel!*

This big sister did a great job of understanding that her sister saw the situation differently. The sister changed how she thought about it and felt and acted with kindness. I bet they got along better for the rest of the day!

In the cartoon, the big sister thought about the situation one way. Then, she was able to see that her sister might think about it differently. Being aware of how her sister was thinking and feeling helped her stop feeling mad. Having empathy helped her calm down and figure out a solution that worked for both of them.

But not everyone can understand others' feelings so easily. Just as some people seem to have been born with the ability to be amazing athletes or wonderful musicians, other people are naturally more able to understand how other people think and feel. Some people, though, need to work hard to figure this out. In the rest of this book, we are going to help you learn more about empathy.

Having empathy can help you:

- feel better;
- manage your feelings when you are upset;
- get along better with your friends and family; and
- get along better with everyone you know.

Once you practice the exercises in this book, we are sure you will get really good at understanding differences. We hope you will treat other people with kindness and they will treat you with kindness too.

Time for a Break!

Can you find the words that are hidden in the word search below?

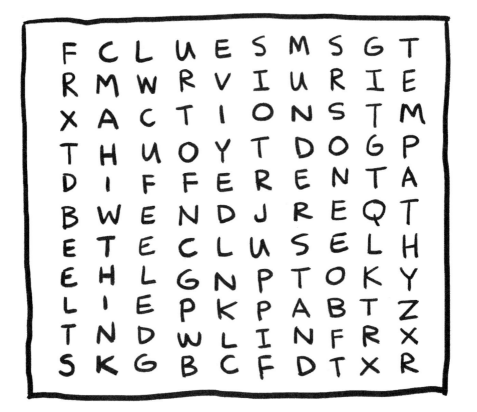

```
F  C  L  U  E  S  M  S  G  T
R  M  W  R  V  I  U  R  I  E
X  A  C  T  I  O  N  S  T  M
T  H  U  O  Y  T  D  O  G  P
D  I  F  F  E  R  E  N  T  A
B  W  E  N  D  J  R  E  Q  T
E  T  E  C  L  U  S  E  L  H
E  H  L  G  N  P  T  O  K  Y
L  I  E  P  K  P  A  B  T  Z
T  N  D  W  L  I  N  F  R  X
S  K  G  B  C  F  D  T  X  R
```

ACTIONS   FEEL
CLUES   THINK
DIFFERENT UNDERSTAND
EMPATHY

CHAPTER TWO

Everyone Sees Things Differently

Turn this picture upside down to see it differently!

There are lots of important things to know about getting along with other kids—and grown-ups, too. The first thing we are going to teach you about is that different people can see the same situation differently. In other words, everyone has his or her own point of view.

Seeing Different Points of View

Have you ever heard the saying, "There are two sides to every coin?" Take out a penny, dime, nickel, or quarter, and you will see that the same coin has two different pictures, one on either side. One side, "heads," has a picture of a face, and the other side, "tails," has a different picture. You and I could both be looking at the same coin. But what if each of us is looking at a different side of the coin and doesn't realize it? If one of us is only looking at the "tails" side and the other is only looking at the "heads" side, we might describe what we're seeing totally differently!

Different people can see the same situation very differently and not realize it.

Here's an example for you to think about.

Look at this delicious piece of cake.

Imagine that you are looking down on it from the top. What shape would you describe?

_____

_____

_____

Now, imagine that your friend is looking at it from the side with the circles. What shape would she describe?

_____

_____

_____

Next, imagine another friend is looking at the darkest side, the one with chocolate sprinkles. What shape is that?

_____

_____

_____

Depending on your point of view, you and your friends might see a triangle, a long rectangle, or a tall rectangle, and you would all be right! But it sure might be confusing if you only saw things from your own point of view. If you can tell each other about your own points of view, there would probably be less confusion—and getting along would be a "piece of cake!"

Feeling Different Points of View

Let's try another example. Have you ever watched a game of soccer? Suppose there's a playing field with goals at either end. Now, imagine a stadium that surrounds the field. Picture lots of fans in the seats. Think about how the field might look depending on where you are sitting.

What might you see if you were sitting near the middle of the field? What about if you were sitting near the end of the field? The field—and the players—would look completely different depending on where you were sitting, wouldn't they?

Now, suppose that one team scores a goal. Some fans and team members will be really happy and cheer loudly. Other fans and team members will be sad or upset.

It's still the same game, isn't it? But different people think and *feel* differently about what happened in the game.

Think about your own experience playing games with your friends. Have you ever played a game with someone, and you were really happy when you won, and he was really sad? Try to remember what game were you playing and the person you were with.

Draw a picture of you and the other person in the first box below. Show what your faces and bodies looked like when you won and the other person lost. Now draw another picture, but change places! Put your friend in your place, and put yourself in your friend's place.

I WON.

MY FRIEND WON.

Take a moment to look at the pictures.
What's different about them?

_____

_____

Take a Break!

Take a look at the bottom picture. What do you think the girl and adult are thinking? Fill in the bubbles with your ideas.

Congratulations! You have taken the first step to getting along well with others, because you are learning how someone else might see a situation. You are beginning to understand that others may have a different point of view from yours—and different feelings about what they see.

CHAPTER THREE

Everyone Shows Their Feelings Differently

HAVE you ever noticed that you can usually tell how an animal is feeling? For example, if you have a dog, does he greet you when you come home from school? Many dogs will run to their family members, wagging their tails and jumping around. They are clearly showing they are excited to see you. It can feel pretty good to get such a nice greeting.

It can be harder to tell how a cat is feeling. If you have a cat, you may notice your cat rubbing against your legs when you come home. That means the cat is happy to see you! Many cats meow and rub up against their owners' legs to indicate that they want to be fed. Have you ever heard a cat purring? When cats purr, it means that they are content and happy.

Some boy animals show off when they are trying to find a girlfriend. For example, peacocks have big tails and feathers; they can spread them out into a big colorful display that stretches across their whole body. That's a pretty good way to impress a girl peacock!

Birds use different sounds in order to talk to each other, tell each other about food, or alert each other to danger. It can be hard to tell what bird calls mean. With other animals, such as fish, gerbils and hamsters, it is even harder to tell what's going on.

Different people show their feelings differently, too. In order to get really good at recognizing what other people are feeling, it is really helpful first to learn about your own feelings.

Take a Break!

Do you have a pet or favorite animal?
Draw a picture of it here.

CHAPTER FOUR

Learn to Recognize What You Are Feeling

BEFORE you can understand someone else's feelings, you need to know more about feelings in general. Let's start with you, since you know yourself better than you know anyone else. Let's talk about some feelings that everyone has.

What are you feeling right now, while you are reading this book? Make a list of words that describe how you feel, or draw a picture of yourself.

Some people think of different feelings as being like different colors; people talk about feeling "blue" when they feel sad or being so mad they could "see red." Do you ever think of your feelings as colors? There are so many feelings people have.

The first step in understanding how others feel is to recognize what you are feeling and thinking. Sometimes it can be really hard to figure out the difference between thoughts and feelings. Let's start with feelings, and then we'll figure out what the thoughts might be that go along with those feelings.

We are going to talk about these feelings:

- Happy
- Surprised
- Afraid
- Angry
- Sad

Of course, there are many more feelings than this, but for now, we are going to concentrate on just a few.

The way you act gives clues about how you feel.

Let's think about changes in your body that tell you that you are feeling happy, surprised, afraid, sad, or mad. We just mentioned that some people think of different feelings as being like different colors. If you think of your feelings as colors, you might want to use colors to draw how you feel.

Happy

Sometimes people talk about feeling like they are "glowing" when they feel happy. They might say they feel like they are "walking on air."

There is a kind of warm feeling that can feel like it takes over your whole body.

You smile a lot and feel like laughing inside and outside.

Do you remember a time when you felt really happy? Draw a picture of yourself and what was happening that day.

What do you remember about what you were thinking when you were feeling really happy? Write down some of your thoughts, or have an adult write them down for you:

_____

_____

_____

Did you notice some changes in your body? What were they? How do you think your face looked?

_____

_____

_____

If you have a color you feel like when you are happy, what color is it?

_____

_____

_____

Surprised

Imagine that it is your birthday. Your friend comes over and asks you to go outside to play. Then when you come back home and walk in the door, a whole bunch of your family and friends are there and they all shout, "Surprise!!" How would you feel? How do you think your face would look?

This is the feeling of surprise. In fact, a party like this is called a "surprise party" because the idea is to do something you didn't expect!

Other kinds of surprises aren't such happy ones. For example, if you slipped on some ice, you might be scared as well as surprised—you didn't see that patch of ice, so you weren't expecting to fall! Some surprises can lead you to feel a nice kind of warm feeling. Other surprises might make you feel kind of scared.

Different people can react differently to surprises. Some people don't like surprise parties at all and feel scared when everyone shouts, "Surprise!" How do you think you would feel? How do you think your body might change? Maybe your eyes and mouth might open really wide, and your heart might start beating fast.

Have you ever felt surprised? What do you remember about what happened to surprise you?

_____

_____

_____

What do you remember about what you were thinking when you were surprised?

_____

_____

_____

Did you notice some changes in your body? Did you feel hot and sweaty all over? Can you imagine what your face looked like?

_____

_____

_____

Write or draw about a time when you felt surprised.

Afraid

Imagine you lived a long, long time ago, when people lived in caves. If you were a caveman who was out walking in the woods and you saw a bear, your brain would send a message to the rest of your body. The message would tell your body to do one of two things—either *run* or *fight for your life*. Your heart would start racing, your breathing would get really fast, and your blood would flow to your muscles, so you would be ready to either run or fight.

You have probably had this feeling sometimes. Maybe your heart was racing and pounding, or your stomach felt kind of strange, like there were butterflies inside. Maybe you felt like you were sweating, or maybe your voice was shaking. This feeling is what we call being afraid.

Sometimes, though, the brain sends a message to your body to *freeze* in place—maybe so the bear won't notice you. Have you ever seen a squirrel freeze in the road when a car drives nearby? It is scared, but it freezes instead of running away.

Nowadays, there aren't many people who have to face a bear. But we still have times when we are afraid—all of us, adults and kids.

Think about a time when you were afraid. What do you remember about what made you afraid?

_____

_____

What do you remember about what you were thinking when you became afraid?

_____

_____

Did you notice some changes in the way your body was acting? What were they? Think about how your heart may have been beating or how you were breathing.

_____

_____

_____

Angry

Let's think again about that caveman walking in the woods and meeting up with a bear. Remember we talked about getting ready to *run* for your life or *fight* for your life or *freeze*? Well, if those messages that your brain sends to the rest of your body are to fight for your life, then you might just be getting ready to be really, really **angry**! You might just get mad enough to fight off that bear (although we know that this wouldn't happen in real life!).

Just like when we are afraid, when we get angry, our hearts race and blood flows quickly to our muscles and our heads. Sometimes, we get red in the face when we get really mad. We may even start to feel hot all over. You might feel yourself start to tremble. You might hear your voice start to shake or get louder. Maybe you clench your fists like you are ready to fight.

Think about a time when you were really angry. What do you remember about why you were angry?

_____

_____

_____

What do you remember about what you were thinking when you were angry?

_____

_____

_____

Did you notice some changes in the way your body was acting? Did you feel hot? Can you imagine what your face looked like?

_____

_____

_____

Sad

Everyone feels sad sometimes. If your friend moves away, or your pet dies, you might feel really sad. People may describe being sad as "having the blues" or being "down in the dumps." Have you ever had a time when you felt really sad?

When some people are sad, they feel like they don't want to do anything. They don't have much energy, and they may think that they'll never be happy again. Some people get angry easily when they are sad. Often people show how they feel with their bodies and faces. They might frown a lot, or they might slump down where they're sitting. They might move really slowly. They may want to be left alone.

If you feel sad a lot of the time, it is really important to tell a grown up.

Have you ever felt really sad like this? What do you remember about what happened?

_____

_____

_____

What do you remember about what you were thinking when you were sad?

_____

_____

_____

Did you notice some changes in your body? What were they?

_____

_____

_____

Take a Break!

Match the feelings on the left with words that describe them on the right.

Surprised	Walking on air
Sad	Eyes and mouth wide open
Happy	Voice is shaking
Angry	Red in the face
Scared	Down in the dumps

CHAPTER FIVE

Learn to Recognize What Others Are Feeling

CONFIDENT

SCARED

ANGRY

SAD

EMBARRASSED

HAPPY

NOW that you are beginning to think about what your body feels like—and what your face might look like—when you have certain feelings, it will be easier for you to recognize when other people have these same feelings.

Once you have some ideas about what other people think and feel, you can check it out. See if you can figure out what someone in your family is feeling, and then ask them.

Here are some ideas to help you.

How Can We Tell What Others Feel?

How can we tell when other people feel happy, surprised, afraid, angry, or sad?

Happy

When people feel happy, they usually have a big smile on their face. Their eyes are bright and shining. They may actually look like they have a bounce in their step when they walk. In the last chapter, we asked you to think about a time when you were really happy. Think about that time now, and go look in the mirror. What do you notice about your face?

Have you ever seen someone you know looking really happy? What happened to make them feel so happy? How did you know they were feeling happy?

Surprised

Remember when we talked about surprises?

Lots of people show surprise by opening their eyes and mouths really wide. They might also put their hands up to their face and shout.

If it is a happy surprise, like getting a present they wanted, they may be smiling a lot, too.

If it is not a nice surprise—for instance, if they accidentally spilled a glass of juice—they might also look sad or mad at the same time they were feeling surprised.

Afraid

How would you know that someone else is feeling afraid? When we talked about feeling afraid earlier, we said that most of the changes that happen in your body are inside.

This is a time to use your *seeing* and *hearing* senses. Try to remember a time when someone you know felt afraid. How did his face look? How did his eyes look? A person's eyes often tell you a lot about what they are feeling. Their eyes might be wide open. How did his mouth look? His mouth might have been open, too! Did he look like he was ready to run or fight? Were his fists tight? Did your ears tell you that his voice was shaky?

To understand other people's thoughts and feelings, try to remember a time when you felt really afraid. Make your face look afraid. Now, look in the mirror. You have a good idea of how someone else might look when he is afraid.

Angry

Think of a time when someone you know was really, really angry. How did you know she was angry? What did you notice about her voice and her face? Did you notice any changes in how she was standing or holding her hands? Maybe her voice got louder and louder, even to the point that she was yelling.

Draw a picture here of a situation that shows someone who is angry.

Sad

How do you know when someone is feeling sad? Have you seen someone when he is sad? When people get sad, they often move slowly. Their eyes don't shine and they may frown a lot. Sometimes when people are sad they might even look angry. They may sit off by themselves, even when there are other people around. Everybody feels sad sometimes.

People Can Have Mixed Feelings

It is also really important to know that people can have more than one feeling at a time! This can make it confusing to understand all the feelings you have. For example, Natasha loved her best friend very much. But sometimes her friend could say mean things that hurt her feelings. Natasha felt confused, sad, and mad every time this happened.

It can also make it confusing to know what other people are feeling. Carlos's older brother Javier was leaving for college. Sometimes Javier yelled, and other times he burst out crying. But when he was packing, he seemed excited. Carlos felt very confused.

Both Natasha and Carlos's brother Javier had mixed feelings—more than one feeling at a time. Maybe you have had experiences when you felt more than one feeling. Mixed feelings can be very confusing.

Write down three things you can look for to tell what another person might be feeling. You might want help from an adult to make this list.

1. _____
_____
_____

2. _____
_____
_____

3. _____
_____
_____

Take a Break!

Can you tell how these kids are feeling? Draw a line to connect each person's face with a feeling word.

EMBARRASSMENT
FEAR
SURPRISE
ANGER
SADNESS
HAPPINESS
CONFUSION
EXCITEMENT

CHAPTER SIX

What Are Thoughts? What Are Feelings?

OFTEN, what we are thinking affects how we are feeling. And how we are thinking and feeling can affect how we treat other people.

Here's an example: Joey was at a play with his family. In the row behind them, a group of people were whispering and talking. Joey thought to himself, "Boy, these people are really annoying. I can't even hear what's going on in the play!" He was thinking he might turn around and say something mean to them.

Then, during a break in the play, Joey heard one of them say, "I am so proud of Sam. I never knew my son could be such a fine actor!" Suddenly, Joey realized that the people in the row behind him were the family of one of the actors on the stage! He thought, "That must be why they are talking and whispering!" He was glad he hadn't said something mean to them. He would have felt bad—and he would have been embarrassed.

Do you see how Joey's feelings changed? When he thought the people behind him were being rude, he was angry.

But when he understood that they were feeling proud—and not trying to be rude—he no longer felt angry. He understood what they were thinking and feeling.

Has anything like this happened to you? Have you ever learned something about someone that completely changed how you thought about them? Did that change your feelings about the person? If this has happened to you, write or draw about it here:

Sometimes we don't understand why people behave the way they do. It is important to try to think of what other people might be thinking and feeling that might be leading them to act the way they do. When you do this, you are "putting yourself in someone else's shoes."

How We Think Affects the Way We Feel

What is a *thought,* and what is a *feeling?*
Understanding the connection between thoughts
and feelings is important. If we can change how we
think, we can change how we feel. It's another way
of being able to put ourselves in someone else's
shoes. If we understand that they might *think* about
things differently than we do, we understand that
they might *feel* differently, too.

Let's think about *thinking* words and *feeling* words.
Go back and take a look at the cartoon about the
sisters in Chapter 1.

Remember when you wrote about the sisters'
thoughts and feelings on page 15? Which words do
you think were thoughts, and which words do you
think were feelings?

Thoughts:

_____

_____

_____

Feelings:

_____

_____

_____

If you wake up in the middle of the night and you hear a noise, you might *feel* scared.

You might *think* that there is something in your room or under your bed.

But what if you *think* that the noise is just wind in the trees or a squirrel outside your house?

Do you see that thinking about things differently can change how you feel? Let's explore this idea some more. In the spaces below, fill in the *thoughts* and *feelings*. Here is an example of what we mean.

What happened:

My mother gave my brother new shoes.

That makes me think:

She likes him better than me.

And then I feel:

I feel sad.

But then I change what I think:

I know she will get me new shoes when

mine are too small.

And then I feel:

I feel better.

Now you try. Think of something that happened to make you feel sad, angry, or scared.

What happened:

_____

That makes me think:

_____

And then I feel:

_____

But then I change what I think:

_____

_____

And then I feel:

_____

Take a Break!

Here is a list of feeling words and thinking words mixed together. Draw a circle around the feeling words. This can be confusing. If you get stuck, check out the answer key at the bottom of the page!

Have fun!

ANNOYED
ANXIOUS
CAN'T
DISAPPOINTED
DISASTER
DON'T
HATE
IRRITATED
LOVE
MUST
NEED
PERFECT
SHOULD
WANT
WORRIED

Answers: annoyed, anxious, disappointed, hate, irritated, love, worried

CHAPTER SEVEN

Why Would Someone Feel This Way?

THINK about some of the feelings we have talked about—happy, surprised, afraid, angry, and sad. Think about when you have had those feelings and what happened that led you to feel that way.

Other people have those feelings, too! Have you ever known someone who was really scared or angry and let you know it?

Write about your experience on the lines below.

Here is what happened:

_____

_____

This is what the other person did:

_____

_____

This is what I think the other person was thinking:

_____

_____

This is what I think the other person was feeling:

_____

_____

Brainstorming About Why Others Feel the Way They Do

Do you remember reading about "brainstorming" in the Introduction? To "brainstorm" means to come up with all the ideas you can think of, without deciding if they right or wrong! You might need a grown-up to help you with this task.

Let's brainstorm to think of as many ideas as we can. Below are some examples of different situations. In each situation, think about:

Thoughts   **Feelings**   **Actions**

- What each person is thinking
- How each person feels
- Then, think about different actions each person could take.
- How would different actions change how the situation turns out?

In the school lunch line, there is one chocolate ice cream left. Joanna, who is first in line, grabs it. Max really wanted it and was counting on having it. What do you think each of them was thinking and feeling?

_____

_____

_____

The class always sits in a circle for reading time. Lila has a chair she always likes to sit in, right in front of the teacher. One day she arrives at the circle to find that Samantha is sitting in her chair. What does Lila think and feel? What might she do?

_____

_____

_____

On the playground at recess, most of the boys are playing soccer. Bianca wants to join them and they won't let her. What do you think the boys might be thinking and feeling? How about Bianca?

_____

_____

_____

The school is putting on a play. There is one lead role for a boy and one for a girl. A whole bunch of kids try out, but only Frankie and Marie get the lead roles. What are some of the thoughts and feelings that the other kids might have?

_____

_____

_____

The more you practice thinking about these different ideas with a grown-up and try them out with someone you trust, the better you will get at it. It will take a lot of practice before you can use these ideas when you are in the middle of a problem. One small step at a time is a good idea, especially when you are learning to put yourself in someone else's shoes!

Showing Empathy Isn't Always Easy!

Feeling empathy for other people can be hard for everyone. Often when we need it most is when we are upset. When we get upset, we can't think very clearly.

When we get upset, the first thing we need to do is to calm down.

Here are some ideas for ways to calm down:

- going outside and taking a walk
- taking some deep breaths
- talking to an adult
- talking to a friend
- listening to music
- writing or drawing about your feelings
- reading a book
- playing a game
- taking a warm shower or bath (if an adult is home)

What are some other ways you can think of to help yourself calm down?

WAYS THAT I CAN CALM DOWN

Once you are calm, you can think better.

Why Can Empathy Be Harder for Some Kids With AD/HD?

Of course, having empathy can be hard for anyone. And it can be especially hard for kids with AD/HD. But empathy is just one of many skills you can learn— and all kids have some things they are really good at! Think about something you enjoy or are good at. Write or draw about it here.

Many kids with AD/HD have trouble keeping their minds on what they want to be doing. Kids with AD/HD sometimes have trouble paying attention to what is happening inside themselves as well as what is happening around them. Sometimes they don't notice how they are feeling inside until it builds up. Not all kids with AD/HD have this problem, but some do.

Also, some kids find that it is really hard to switch activities—to stop thinking about one thing and change to thinking about something else. Sometimes, your brain can get stuck on an idea and it can be hard to get unstuck. If you are kind of stuck thinking and feeling one way, it can be hard to switch to thinking about someone else's point of view.

Kids with AD/HD can also have difficulty with trying to remember and do many things at the same time. Does that sound familiar? Organizing all these thoughts and feelings and deciding how to act is a lot to ask of anyone!

Just like some math problems have lots of steps, there are many steps involved in getting along with other people. When you do a complicated math problem, you have to remember what you are doing, what you have already done, and what you still need to do. That's a lot like the steps you have to take to have empathy.

Here's a short list to help you remember:

- Stop and cool down.
- Remember that everyone sees things differently.
- Ask: What am I feeling?
- Ask: What are my thoughts about what happened?
- Ask: What clues do I have about what the other person is feeling?
- Brainstorm with an adult or a friend about how the other person might think about the situation.

If you do all these things, you are taking steps toward having empathy for what someone else is thinking and feeling.

Wow! That's a lot of stuff to remember! It's no wonder this is such a challenge. We want you to know that getting along with others is hard for most people. And keep in mind that kids usually get better at having empathy as they grow up and their brains grow, too!

Take a Break!

Follow this maze through the steps to get to empathy.

CHAPTER EIGHT

Putting It All Together

IN the previous chapter, we mentioned the first six steps to learning about empathy:

- Stop and cool down.
- Remember that everyone sees things differently.
- Ask: What am I feeling?
- Ask: What are my thoughts about what happened?
- Ask: What clues do I have about what the other person is feeling?
- Brainstorm with an adult or a friend about how the other person might think about the situation.

Now you are ready for some problem-solving. Think about a problem you have had with someone else. You may wish to do this next step with an adult.

- Are there some other ways that you can think about what happened?
- Does that change how you feel?
- What were your choices about how to act?
- What do you think would happen after each response?
- What's the best choice?

Remember that the way you act will affect how the other person thinks and feels and how they will treat you—which, in turn, will affect how you feel.

Imagine that instead of getting mad, Luis thinks, "Hey, this makes it look kind of cool!" What might have happened?

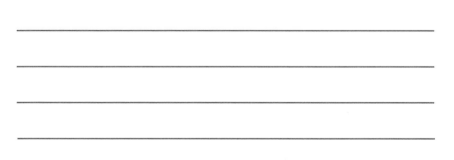

Think about treating other people the way you want others to treat you. Sometimes we call this idea the "Golden Rule." If you can see things from another person's point of view and understand how they think and feel, then perhaps you will be better able to treat them as you would want to be treated. You will find that you will get along better with other people, and they will probably treat you better!

Here are some examples of kids who used these ideas to help them get along with other people.

With Family

Keyisha is Sakinah's big sister. She is two years older. Their bedrooms are right next to each other. Both girls like to borrow clothes from each other since they are the same size and like the same clothes. But sometimes Sakinah forgets to return the clothes she borrowed, or she gives them back dirty. Keyisha gets really mad and yells at Sakinah. Then Sakinah runs crying to their mom. Their parents get involved and both sisters end up getting punished, which Keyisha doesn't think is fair.

What do you think they could do differently?

_____

_____

_____

Here's what their parents figured out. They decided to sit down with both girls and talk about borrowing clothes. They talked about the reasons why it was a good idea; each girl got twice the amount of clothes for the same amount of money!

First, their parents asked Sakinah to go into Keyisha's room (with her permission, of course). They asked her to look over all her clothes and to see exactly what she had returned with spots on

it. They asked her to talk about how Keyisha might think about this situation. What if she really wanted to wear that shirt tomorrow morning and it was dirty? What might she think, and how might she feel?

Sakinah took a little while to think and said that she thought Keyisha might be really disappointed. She might think that Sakinah was being selfish. Sakinah began to see why Keyisha was so upset. She picked up Keyisha's clothes and put them in the laundry. She said she was sorry and would try to do better.

Next, their mom asked Keyisha to think about why Sakinah might be having this problem. She asked Keyisha to stand in Sakinah's room and to think about why Sakinah might borrow her clothes and forget to get them cleaned before giving them back. She saw that Sakinah's room was a mess, and there was no laundry basket!

Their mom suggested that perhaps instead of yelling at Sakinah, Keyisha could help her organize the room and could give Sakinah one of the laundry baskets from her room. Everyone agreed this was a better solution than yelling and fighting. Sakinah apologized and promised to use the laundry basket, and Keyisha accepted her apology.

Going into another person's room and taking things without asking might cause someone to have certain thoughts and feelings. How do you think you would feel if someone took some of your things without asking? Write about those feelings here.

With Friends

Megan was having a wonderful time at the beach with her family. She and her little sister Leah were playing in the sand. Suddenly Megan said, "Let's build a pool out of sand, so we can cool ourselves off whenever we want!" Leah thought it was a great idea and they begin to dig. They worked hard; first they found a great spot where the water made a tide pool on the beach. They built a dam so the water couldn't flow back into the sea. Then they started digging.

Meanwhile just down the beach, two boys were playing in the sand. They were also building something. One of them came over while Megan and Leah were busy working. He said, "You have to move your dam down the beach because we need the space." It turned out that they were building a sand pool, too!

At first Megan got really mad. She thought to herself, "Those boys are being really mean. How dare they tell us we have to move our sand pool because they needed the water for theirs! Who do they think they are, anyway?" Megan went into the water to cool down and think.

After she cooled off and took some time to think about her feelings, she thought, "Those boys just want to do the same thing Leah and I want to do.

They didn't ask very nicely. But they look like good diggers, too. I wonder if we could build a bigger and better sand pool if we worked together."

So she went back and talked to them. The boys liked her idea. All four of them dug and dug and worked and worked and were really building a nice sand pool in the sand with a great dam to block the water. The boys were good diggers, and Megan and Leah were good builders. The sand pool was built in no time at all.

They all jumped in, splashing around and having a great time. Later on, Megan thought of a saying her dad had often shared with her: "When life gives you lemons, make lemonade." That means you can take something unpleasant and turn it into something sweet or pleasing. And she felt really proud of herself for doing just that.

What were the "lemons" in this situation? How did Megan practice empathy? She calmed herself down so she could think less about her own feelings and more about what the boys might be thinking and feeling. Once she did that, she was able to solve the problem by having everyone work together. Way to go, Megan!

At School

David had trouble reading. He got really embarrassed in school when the teacher asked him to read out loud. He stumbled over the words and read them wrong or couldn't read them at all. He felt really stupid. The other kids in the class called him names, and it made him feel really bad about himself and very sad.

David started to feel like he didn't want to go to school. His mom and dad asked him what was wrong, and he finally told them that he felt really stupid when the teachers called on him to read out loud in front of the class. He explained that the letters were all blurry and he couldn't see them very well.

His parents took him to the eye doctor, who figured out that David had trouble seeing and that was why the words were all blurry. No wonder David couldn't read out loud; he couldn't see the words on the page! So the doctor gave David glasses.

David's teacher wanted to help his classmates understand what David was thinking and feeling about this situation. She found some reading pages that were blurry. She gave them out to the class and asked them to read out loud. She went around the room. Each of David's classmates had to try to read these blurry pages, and they couldn't do it. The teacher asked the children what it felt like to have to try to read these blurry pages.

Next, she explained that this was what happened to people when they can't see very well. She explained that we have to be careful about teasing other people and calling them names, because usually there is a good reason why people have trouble doing some things like reading.

Take a Break!

Have you ever been made fun of? What was the situation, and how did you feel? What did you think? Write or draw about this here.

Have you ever made fun of someone else? How do you think that person felt? What do you think they thought about you, and how do you think they felt about you? Write or draw about this here.

A Final Message to You

You have done a great job! You have learned that people see things from different points of view. They can think and feel differently even about the same event. You have learned ways to help you understand more about how you think and feel. You have also learned some ideas to help you be able to understand how other people think and feel.

Once you understand these differences, you can choose how to act toward other people. You can think about how your actions affect other people and how their actions can then affect you. By understanding differences, you can choose to treat people with kindness. Hopefully, they will treat you with kindness as well.

You can put yourself in another person's shoes and imagine how they think and feel. This will help you get along with other people at home, at school, and in your neighborhood.

Here are thoughts to remember:

E: **E**veryone sees things differently.

M: **M**y Feelings—I can learn to recognize and label them.

P: **P**oint of view—How I see things affects how I feel. How other people see things affects how they feel.

A: **A**sk yourself—What clues do I see or hear that show me how another person feels?

T: **T**reat others the way I want to be treated.

H: **H**ow I act affects how other people treat me and how I feel.

Y: **Y**es—I can put myself in someone else's shoes and understand how they think and feel!

CONGRATULATIONS! You have taken important steps in building your empathy skills to help you feel good about yourself and get along better with other people. These steps will help you with your friends, your family, and everyone you know—today, tomorrow, and throughout the rest of your life.

Note To Parents

Working Together to Make Changes

As you have learned, there are different aspects of what we call empathy:

- The ability to see things from another person's point of view
- The ability to feel what another person is feeling
- The ability to imagine what it might be like to be another person and to put yourself in someone else's shoes

Let's think about some ways you can work together with your children to help them, and let's add more ideas to what you've discovered.

The ability to see things from another person's point of view

- Looking at an optical illusion is a great way to understand that people see things differently. On the Internet, search "optical illusions, images" to find a variety. Ask your child what he or she sees, and share what you see. Ask your child which one is a favorite, and share your favorite.

- Talk about sporting events or other activities you are watching. Talk with your child about what it might feel like to be some of the people you are watching.

The ability to feel what another person is feeling

- Imagine that you are experiencing a strong feeling, such as anger, frustration, or sadness. Show one of these emotions on your face, and ask your child if she can look at you and guess what you are feeling. Then, ask what she might do to help you if you were experiencing one of these feelings.

- You can also play a game with your children. One person can call out a suggestion, such as "Make a face like you just fell in the mud," and then everyone else shows that facial expression.

- Look in a mirror with your child. Try on different emotions by thinking about different things that make you feel sad, happy, angry, disgusted, or surprised. Share what you both look like when you are feeling these emotions. See if you and your child can identify changes in your faces when you think about situations that cause you to feel particular emotions.

The ability to imagine what it might be like to be another person and to put yourself in someone else's shoes

- When you are outside your home, imagine other people's life stories with your children. What is each person's story? Make something up together. How are they feeling, and what might they be thinking? How might their lives be different than your own?

- If your children are fighting, or your child is fighting with a friend, sit down with them to talk about what is happening. Let the children know that you would like to hear what each child is thinking and feeling. Tell them that each of them will have two minutes to say everything they think and feel, while you and the other child listen without interrupting. Then, let the other child do the same thing. Next, have them change seats. See if they can tell what the other person had to say. Try to get each child to say what he is thinking and what he is feeling. (It can be hard for kids with AD/HD to sit still for two minutes, so you might have to start with one minute.)

- When a family problem arises, have everyone go to a quiet place to calm down. Then, have a family meeting at a later time. Have each family member take five minutes to talk about how they saw the situation and how they felt. Each person should have a chance to talk without being interrupted. An agreement has to be made that everyone will listen respectfully to each other. Go around again if you need to, so everyone gets to give their point of view. Try to make the meeting pleasant and positive—serving snacks can sometimes help.

- Michelle Garcia Winner, MA, CCC-SLP, has developed excellent resources and strategies to help children understand their social lives. She has a tremendous amount of information available on her website: www.socialthinking .com. Ms. Winner suggests pausing TV shows and movies to talk with your child about what the different characters might be thinking and feeling. She also suggests talking about characters in books and their different points of view.

- A program called *Roots of Empathy* has been developed by Mary Gordon for use in the classroom. In this program, a mom and baby visit a classroom every month or so during a school year. During these regular visits, the children are asked questions like, "If the baby could talk, what would she say?" In addition, the children watch as the mother reads the baby's nonverbal cues to try to figure out what the baby wants when she cries. As the children in the class interact with the baby over time, they improve their abilities to communicate. This program teaches children to understand and label their own emotions, as well as those of other people.

- With your child, volunteer at a senior citizens' center or a local food bank. Ask some of the people there to tell you about themselves, and listen to what they say. If you are not comfortable asking them, wait until you have left, and then you and your child can discuss what their lives might be like. Some senior citizens' centers have photos of people at different stages of their lives and of their families that can help you get started.
- Have your child interview family members about their life stories. It's easy to forget that he doesn't know much about how grandma and grandpa grew up or met each other. An interview can shed light about the happy times and challenges they have faced, as well as how their thoughts and feelings have grown and changed over the years. Go to storycorps.org to explore some interesting family interviews and discover ideas about how to interview family members.

Now that we've given you a jump start, you can probably think of several other ideas to help you and your child understand how other people think and feel. Your ideas may even work better than our suggestions, because they come from you and are therefore more meaningful to you and your child.

Sometimes families need help with having conversations about feelings and different points of view, especially when there is tension involved. Family therapy can be a very useful way to address these kinds of situations. Here are some places to locate a therapist:

- American Psychological Association (www.apa.org)

- National Register of Health Care Providers in Psychology (www.findapsychologist.org)

- American Association for Marriage and Family Therapy (www.aamft.org)

- National Association of Social Workers (www.naswdc.org)

Create a Plan of Action

Would you and your child like to improve your ability to understand how other people think and feel? Are there some ways you would like to improve how the members of your family get along with each other? Perhaps you can even get the whole family involved in some fun projects. Talk to your child and see if she would like to work on one of these ideas. Write them here.

_____

_____

_____

_____

Next, write about some situations where you would like to see both your child and yourself improve your ability to see things from another person's point of view and to understand how others think and feel.

_____

_____

_____

_____

Then think about where along the line your child might be able to make some changes, so there is a different outcome than in the past.

It is very important to remember and to tell your child that he can't change how other people act; the only person he can change is himself.

Set aside time to do these activities. Choose only one at a time to work on—it is difficult to focus on changing more than one behavior at a time. You might write them on a calendar.

A few weeks later, look back at the first set of ideas you wrote down on the previous page—the areas you wanted to improve upon. Have you noticed any changes? Be sure to reward your children— and yourself!—for all of the positive changes you have noticed.

Resources

For Parents, Counselors, and Teachers

Online Resources

Children and Adults With Attention-Deficit/Hyperactivity Disorder: www.chadd.org

Daniel Goleman: www.danielgoleman.info

The Gottman Institute: www.gottman.com

Social Thinking: www.socialthinking.com

Books

Dunn Buron, K., & Curtis, M. (2012). *The incredible 5-point scale: Assisting students in understanding social interactions and controlling their emotional responses* (2nd ed.). Shawnee Mission, KS: AAPC.

Caselman, T. (2007). *Teaching children empathy, the social emotion: Lessons, activities and reproducible worksheets (K–6) that teach how to "step into others' shoes."* Chapin, SC: YouthLight.

Goleman, D. (2005). *Emotional intelligence: Why it can matter more than IQ.* (10th anniversary ed.) New York, NY: Bantam Books.

Goleman, D. (2011). *The brain and emotional intelligence: New insights.* Northampton, MA: More Than Sound.

Gordon, M. (2009). *The roots of empathy: Changing the world child by child.* New York, NY: The Experiment.

Gottman, J. (with Declaire, J.). (1998). *Raising an emotionally intelligent child: The heart of parenting.* New York, NY: Simon & Schuster.

Lantieri, L. (2008). *Building emotional intelligence: Techniques to cultivate inner strength in children.* Boulder, CO: Sounds True.

Shapiro, L. (2008). *Learning to listen, learning to care: A workbook to help kids learn self-control and empathy.* Oakland, CA: Instant Help Books.

Siegel, D. J. (2010). *Mindsight: The new science of personal transformation.* New York, NY: Bantam Books.

Siegel, D. J. (2012). *The whole-brain child: 12 revolutionary strategies to nurture your child's developing mind.* New York, NY: Bantam Books.

Winner, M. G. (2007). *Thinking about you thinking about me* (2nd ed.). San Jose, CA: Think Social.

For Kids

Movie

Pixar Animation Studios. (2015). *Inside out* [Motion picture].

The opening line of the film is: "Do you ever look at someone and wonder what is going on inside their head?" The plot line follows the thoughts and feelings of an 11-year-old girl as she struggles to cope with a major life change—a family move. At times, the movie also reveals the thoughts and feelings of other people, including her mother and father. While it is a somewhat complicated plot for young children, many thought-provoking ideas are presented for follow-up discussion with parents or other adults.

Books

DeBell, S. (2006). *How do I stand in your shoes?* Chapin, SC: YouthLight.

Glasser, J. & Nadeau, K. (2014). *Learning to feel good and stay cool: Emotional regulation tools for kids with AD/HD.* Washington, DC: Magination Press.

Sornson, R. (2013). *Stand in my shoes: Kids learning about empathy.* Golden, CO: Love and Logic.

Winner, M. G. (2008). *You are a social detective.* San Jose, CA: Think Social.

About the Authors

Judith M. Glasser, PhD, is a clinical psychologist who has worked with children and their families for over 30 years. She specializes in the assessment and treatment of AD/HD in children. For many years Dr. Glasser has been interested in the different kinds of difficulties children experience when they have AD/HD. Many of the children she works with have difficulty understanding how other people think and feel; this book is for them. Dr. Glasser is also the author, with Kathleen Nadeau, PhD, of *Learning to Feel Good and Stay Cool* (Magination Press, 2014).

Jill Menkes Kushner, MA, is an educational and editorial professional, currently working in the College Board's Advanced Placement Assessments division. Ms. Kushner has an extensive background as a writer and editor for curriculum and assessment products in all subjects, specializing in English/Language Arts. Her publications include several periodicals and the following books: *The Farming Industry* (Franklin Watts, 1984), *Who on Earth is Dian Fossey?: Defender of the Mountain Gorilla* (Enslow Publishers, Inc., 2009), and *Johnny Depp* (Enslow Publishers, Inc., 2009).

About the Illustrator

Charles Beyl creates humorous illustrations for books, magazines, and newspapers from his studio high atop a nineteenth-century Pennsylvania farmhouse.

About Magination Press

Magination Press is an imprint of the American Psychological Association, the largest scientific and professional organization representing psychologists in the United States and the largest association of psychologists worldwide.